WAYS CHILDREN
LEARN

WAYS CHILDREN LEARN

What Do Experts Say?

By

GEETA R. LALL, Ph.D.

*Educational Diagnostician, Learning Disabilities Consultant
and Remedial Curriculum Specialist
Berrien Springs — Benton Harbor, Michigan*

and

BERNARD M. LALL, Ph.D.

*Professor of Educational Administration
Andrews University
Berrien Springs, Michigan*

With a Foreword by

Robert J. Havighurst, Ph.D.

*Professor of Education and Human Development
University of Chicago
Chicago, Illinois*

CHARLES C THOMAS • PUBLISHER

Springfield • Illinois • U.S.A.

Published and Distributed Throughout the World by
CHARLES C THOMAS • PUBLISHER
2600 South First Street
Springfield, Illinois, 62717, U.S.A.

© *1983 by* CHARLES C THOMAS • PUBLISHER
ISBN 0-398-04754-5
Library of Congress Catalog Card Number: 82-10578

With THOMAS BOOKS *careful attention is given to all details of manufacturing and
design. It is the Publisher's desire to present books that are satisfactory as to their physical
qualities and artistic possibilities and appropriate for their particular use.* THOMAS
BOOKS *will be true to those laws of quality that assure a good name and good will.*

Printed in the United States of America
CU-R-1

Library of Congress Cataloging in Publication Data
Lall, Geeta Rani, 1934-
    Ways children learn.

    Bibliography: p.
    Includes index.
    1. Learning. 2. Education--Philosophy.
3. Educators. I. Lall, Bernard M., 1929-
II. Title.
LB1060.L34   1982   370.15'23   82-10578
ISBN 0-398-04754-5

This book is fondly and respectfully dedicated to one of the eminent educators we have ever known. He not only taught us communicative skills and administrative theory and practice, but also instilled in us a hunger for knowledge and a real sense of joy in becoming effective educators.

Above all, like all his students the world over, we consider him a true friend. He is none other than Dr. Ivan D. Higgins, former president of Spicer Memorial College, where both of us had the privilege of completing our teacher education program.

Geeta Rani Lall
Bernard M. Lall

FOREWORD

THIS book gives a useful summary of facts and theories concerning the learning process in early and middle childhood.

The authors of the book, Geeta R. and Bernard M. Lall, analyzed and summarized the work of eight people, each of whom has created a systematic procedure for organizing the curriculum and classroom teaching methods for children from kindergarten to age ten or twelve. Six of the eight are Americans who are now living. In addition there are two Europeans — Maria Montessori and Jean Piaget, now deceased.

Jerome Bruner is presented first, with his basic proposition that "any subject can be taught effectively in some intellectually honest form to any child at any stage of development."

Each of the eight people whose work is presented was interested in the preschool years as well as the elementary school years. Special note should be made of the work of Burton White, the Director of the Preschool Project of the Harvard University School of Education.

The book will be useful as a supplement to a text on Educational Psychology. It will be good for classroom teachers and for curriculum specialists.

Robert J. Havighurst

PREFACE

WAYS CHILDREN LEARN is a theoretical discourse. It presents concepts from outstanding authorities who have for many years provided knowledge in the field of learning.

It would be difficult to cover each aspect of the various theories of learning in a single book. What we have done is to provide glimpses into the theories that have significant effect on learning. It is hoped that the reader will find these glimpses interesting enough to explore further in the field, for it is our belief that as the scientists of our day continue to study learning theories, new and visionary concepts will emerge.

We were first asked by the World Council for Curriculum and Instruction (WCCI) to prepare a paper on this topic to be presented at the world congress held at Istanbul, Turkey. The paper generated much interest among scholars from many parts of the world and copies were sought for distribution. Therefore, we have researched and revised further in order to develop this material. Now we are ready to share with educators everywhere the insights we have gained in the *Ways Children Learn*.

Geeta R. Lall
Bernard M. Lall

ACKNOWLEDGMENTS

IN writing a book one depends on so many people for help, it is difficult to mention each one by name. Furthermore, we fully realize that each word we ever write is not our own — someone painstakingly taught us these words. Therefore, it becomes increasingly difficult to list the names of all who one way or another helped us in writing this book.

However, there are several persons we should like to remember in acknowledging their help and support. They are Maurice Dupreez, Cheryl Hunter, Jaycee Palmer, and Renata K. Bokpe for their assistance in putting this book together. To them we offer our gratitude and heartfelt thanks.

G.R.L.
B.M.L.

CONTENTS

WAYS CHILDREN
LEARN

Chapter 1

LEARNING PERSPECTIVE

MARY, a five-year-old, was a marvel to her parents, grandparents, and the educators in the community because she could read story books generally read by elementary and junior high school students. What was more spectacular, though, was Mary's ability to read at the eighth grade level and she had never attended school — even for a day!

"Mary, come here to the table and read for these folks," called her mother when we visited her home. Presently, Mary came scurrying into the room. Reaching for the eighth grade science textbook, Mary's mother asked her to read to us. Mary read clearly and distinctly without a bit of hesitation, except that she had difficulty with the pronunciation of *one* scientific term on that whole page!

We were amazed! How could a five-year-old child, who had never attended kindergarten or formal school, read at the eighth-grade level when there were scores of children who experienced great difficulty in reading at their own grade level? We asked the child's mother to tell us how Mary had learned to read so well. She reflected for a moment, then said, "It began when Mary was two years old. She would sit at breakfast and ask me what was written on the cereal boxes. Starting with the large, bold letters, I would read to her, and she would repeat what I said. That's how she learned to read." We also found out that this gifted girl was always asking questions, ever seeking to satisfy her curiosity. Whenever she and her mother drove downtown, Mary wanted to know what was written on each billboard. Moreover, when any word was pronounced or uttered just once, Mary could repeat it without trouble.

From this story it can be seen that Mary learned to read through visual and auditory methods. More interesting is the fact that she learned to read at the eighth-grade level from her mother who took enough interest to tell her daughter what each word was, defined its meaning, and demonstrated how to pronounce it correctly.

Educators should remember, however, that although Mary has learned to read through visual and auditory processes, all children will not learn to read in exactly the same way. Therefore, one of the early steps that a teacher must take is to discover the ways in which each child learns best. Learning is an individualized process.

In a study conducted by the Socony-Mobil Oil Company, some very interesting information was obtained on how people learn. One percent learn through taste; 1 to 1.5 percent through touch; 3 to 3.5 percent through smell; 11 percent through hearing; and 83 percent through sight (see Table I).

Table I

HOW PEOPLE LEARN

Learning Mode	Percentage
Through taste	1
Through touch	1-1.5
Through smell	3-3.5
Through hearing	11
Through sight	83

It is also interesting to note that the retention factor is different on the basis of the method used to learn. According to the Socony-Mobil Oil Company study, children retain 10 percent of what they read; 20 percent of what they hear; 30 percent of what they see; 50 percent of what they see and hear simultaneously; 70 percent of what they say; and 90 percent of what they say and do at the same time (see Table II). Perhaps this is why the "show and tell" period in the early grades is so popular with children.

Table II

RETENTION PATTERNS

Retention Mode	Percentage
What is read	10
What is heard	20
What is seen	30
What is seen and heard simultaneously	50
What is verbalized	70
What is said and done at the same time	90

Another interesting factor is the time span of retention. It appears that children recall more after a time span when they have used the multisensory approach in

Table III

RETENTION TIME SPAN

Instructional Method	Recall 3 hours later Percentage	Recall 3 days later Percentage
A blend of showing (or demonstrating) and lecturing	85	65
Showing (or demonstrating only)	72	20
Lecture method	70	10

learning. When a combination of showing and telling is used, children tend to remember 85 percent three hours later, and 65 percent three days later. What we are proposing to all educators is the fact that children will retain more if a multisensory approach is used in the teaching-learning situation rather than a monosensory approach (see Table III).

WHICH CHILDREN SUCCEED

We have already noted that what is said and done at the same time has the highest percentage of retention (90%). It appears that the value of practical aspect of learning cannot be overemphasized. There is another important aspect of learning and success worthy of our consideration. A child that is industrious (more than his intelligence, family background, and social class) will become a productive and emotionally healthy adult.

A study conducted by Harvard University professor of psychiatry, Dr. George E. Valliant, and Caroline O. Valliant, a social worker at the same university, shows that a child's willingness and capacity to work is the most important factor in predicting his productive adult life (Cole, 1982).

Parents should provide simple tasks for children at an early age. As early as possible, a child should be able to put toys neatly away with the help of the parents. This is a good beginning. Reinforcement such as a hug or a thank you at the conclusion of the task provides encouragement and motivation for the child to want to do the task again. As the child increases in wisdom and stature, the tasks also can be increased. Dr. Cynthia Shilkret, a clinical psychologist, says, "Don't baby the child, but don't expect him to do something beyond his years, either. . . ." Dr.

Robert Shilkret points out that the parents should provide room for failure and should not humiliate the child because of unsuccessful trial (Cole, 1982).

Gently, encouragingly allow the child to complete his task. Do not overburden the child with too much work or work that is too menial. A child is willing to follow example of parents in doing household jobs. It can be so much fun for children to help their parents with daily chores!

As children grow older and commence formal schooling, a work-study philosophy of education should be adopted. Students who work their way through school appear to do better academic work and enjoy a more productive adult life physically, emotionally, and socially. They seem to have greater commitment toward their immediate society, country, and the world at large.

When they choose to undertake a work-study program, students reap a range of values and skills. In general, they "naturally and effectively learn dependability, responsibility, order, neatness, industry, initiative, cleanliness, and sound work habits" (Moore, 1976). They feel needed and have a sense of service, which induces an all-important sense of self-worth. In developing a value system, the student works together with the teacher; this produces "patience, kindness, understanding, tact, forgiveness, and forebearance. . . ." (Moore, 1976). With a balanced work program, students also become self-disciplined. However, "one of the clearest outcomes from balanced work-study programs is the overall, general increase in academic achievement. Human reason does not always quickly grasp the fact that students learn more with less study. Nevertheless it is true. The physiological support of a healthy body provides the brain with the vital energy it needs to work at a superior level" (Moore). Also, the student develops a better appreciation for the need of a formal education as it relates to work.

WHAT EXPERTS TELL US

We are going to review some of the approaches suggested by experts in the field of education and psychology regarding their concepts on ways children learn. The works of the following people will be reviewed: Jerome Bruner, Benjamin Bloom, Lawrence Kohlberg, Robert Havighurst, Maria Montessori, Jean Piaget, Burton White, and Terrel Bell.

It is our hope that guidelines, dealing with the ways children learn, may be developed for better teaching-learning practices.

Chapter 2

JEROME BRUNER

Jerome S. Bruner is Professor of Psychology at Harvard University, where he was founder and Director of the Center for Cognitive Studies. Professor Bruner received his B.A. degree from Duke University and his Ph.D. degree from Harvard. For some time now, Dr. Bruner's interest in the cognitive processes has centered in the development of children and the nature of the educational process. Dr. Bruner has served on numerous academic and governmental advisory boards and holds honorary degrees from an array of prestigious universities. Dr. Bruner is also a prolific author and has contributed immensely to the expanding knowledge in the field of cognitive development. Among his publications are **The Process of Education, A Study of Thinking, Studies of Cognitive Growth,** *and* **Toward A Theory of Instruction.**

BRUNER once said, "Any subject can be taught effectively in some intellectually honest form to any child at any stage of development." One needs to study his concepts of cognitive growth in order to fully understand why Bruner believed in the above proposition.

"Instrumental conceptualization" is a term that aptly describes Bruner's theory. He proposes the idea that knowledge of the world is formed on a constructed model of reality. This model of reality is constructed from experiences, the concept of time, space, and cause and effect. The ultimate result of a constructed model of the world is greatly shaped by three steps or stages: (1) action, (2) imagery, and (3) symbolism (Bruner, 1966 A).

9

ACTION: Action, or the enactive stage, is primarily manipulative; one is bound by the physical properties of one's world. At this stage, the mind only works effectively on one track. The small child only deals with one thought process at a time. In the action stage, the child has a short attention span and learns almost completely by doing.

IMAGERY: Imagery, the second stage, called iconic representation by Bruner, is when the child begins to build a mental picture of the way in which things function. Past experiences are developed into images. The child's understanding of concepts is facilitated by these images, which, however, does not specifically define the concepts.

SYMBOLISM: In the third stage, the child develops the ability to look for different options. When faced with a problem, he can consider all the alternatives before coming up with a solution. He is able to verbally define a concept instead of just drawing a mental picture of it. He is also able to verbalize his knowledge of the concept in such a way as to make it understandable to others.

From the founding of the "model of reality," the growth process is shaped by the experiences the culture involves the individual in and by the individual's needs. A child grows by the process of internalizing the ways of acting, imagining, and symbolizing that exist in his culture, ways that amplify his powers (Bruner, 1966 A).

These powers in turn are developed according to the individual's use of them throughout his life. Bruner believes that there are three factors in our lives upon which the development of these powers depends: (1) the supply of images, conceptions, and skills in the individual's culture; (2) the type of life the individual leads; (3) how much a person is motivated to use his three modes of knowing — action, image, and symbol — and how much he explores the interrelationships of these three modes (Bruner, 1966 A).

Bruner explains that we really know very little of how the first two factors affect an individual. Traditions and mores definitely vary from culture to culture. Even in a culture where a tradition or skill is very highly developed, it may not affect every individual in that culture. Quite possibly, a whole segment of the culture may not be affected by that tradition at all.

Schooling forms the main part of the third factor. In the western culture, it is in the school setting where the child is actually "forced" to suitably rearrange and possibly restructure his knowledge so that he may code it for verbalization. The coding not only makes it easier for the child to understand himself but also for others to understand him (Bruner, 1966 A).

The importance of "discovery" as a motivational factor in learning is emphasized by Bruner. A child, as he begins to understand a concept, goes through the same three stages that helped him form his concept of reality. First, his actions are manipulative. Next, imagery sets in, and the child begins to understand how the concept "works." Lastly, he understands the concept so well that he can verbally define it.

IMPLICATIONS OF THEORY
TO PRACTICAL APPLICATION

Jerome Bruner saw the spiral curriculum as the practical application of his theory. He sees the proper emphasis of education as the transmission of skills and that a complex skill can be viewed as composed of a set of simpler constituent skills. If such constituent skills are taught in the early stages of education, they may be combined more readily into their complex forms later on. Bruner thus sees the task of the parent/teacher as that of converting knowledge into a form that fits growing minds. The material to be transmitted should be tailored, sequenced, and embodied in a form appropriate to the learner's developmental level. Two recurrent themes in Bruner's cognitive psychology have been crucial in shaping his view of education. The first is the notion that the acquisition of knowledge is an active process. Therefore the student should be encouraged to work things out for himself, organize evidence so that he is able to go beyond it to novel conjectures and insights, and participate in active dialogue with his teacher. A second related theme is that when a person actively constructs knowledge, he does so by relating incoming information to a previously acquired psychological frame of reference, which gives meaning and organization to experiences and allows the individual to go beyond the information given.

Several practical implications of Bruner's theory for the classroom follow:

A. Exploration of Alternatives — since learning and problem-solving depend upon the exploration of alternatives, instruction must facilitate and regulate this activity. Such activity requires
   1. Something to get it started — a degree of uncertainty and/or ambiguity. A cut and dried routine task provokes little exploration; one that is too uncertain may arouse confusion and anxiety.
   2. Something to keep it going — this requires that the benefits from exploring alternatives exceed the risks incurred. Thus the consequences of error or wrong alternatives should be less serious and nonthreatening.

3. Something to keep it from being random — this necessitates a sense of the goal/purpose of a task and a knowledge of the relevance of tested alternatives to the achievement of that goal/purpose.

B. Sequence and Its Uses — the sequence in which a learner encounters materials affects the difficulty he will have in achieving mastery. There is no sequence common to all learners and the optimum in any particular case depends on many factors, such as past learning, stage of development, nature of the material, and individual differences. A spiral curriculum, which would follow cognitive developmental theory, would begin with action, move to visual or other sensory representation, and culminate in symbolic representation.

C. Form and Pacing of Reinforcement — learning depends upon knowledge of results at a time when and at a place where the knowledge can be used for correction. Knowledge of results should come at that point in a problem-solving episode when the learner is comparing the results of his try-out with some criterion of what he seeks to achieve. The knowledge of results must also provide information as to whether the particular act is in fact leading the learner through the hierarchy of goals he is trying to achieve.

In summary, Bruner feels that if a curriculum and teacher are to be effective in the classroom, both must have various ways of activating/motivating children, numerous types of sequences, and flexibility for some children to skip parts while others work their way through. A curriculum and a teacher must allow for many routes leading to the same goal.

Chapter 3

BENJAMIN BLOOM

Benjamin S. Bloom is Distinguished Service Professor of Education at the University of Chicago and one of our most eminent educational scholars and writers. He is the author or co-author of a number of major books, including **Taxonomy of Educational Objectives, Stability and Change in Human Characteristics,** *and* **Handbook of Formative and Summative Evaluation of Student Learning.** *Dr. Bloom is one of the founding members of the International Association for the Evaluation of Educational Achievement and has been a consultant on evaluation and curriculum to nations throughout the world. He is a past president of the American Educational Research Association.*

BLOOM is a proponent of the view that the environment affects a young child's intelligence. He states that in the behavioral sciences, the most important research problems deal with early learning in children and the effects of the environment during those formative years (Bloom, 1964). Perhaps the key concept presented by him is the Mastery Learning.

Bloom's longitudinal studies are based on factors that may be either helpful or detrimental in determining the development of general intelligence. According to him, all individuals are born with a physiological and neurological makeup upon which the development of general intelligence is based. Since most individuals vary in their makeup, these differences are important factors in determining the individual's potential for general intel-

15

lectual development (Bloom, 1964).

In his book, *Stability and Change in Human Characteristics,* Bloom discusses the correlation between height at a given age and height at maturity. The analysis of this correlation, according to Bloom, should help in finding the tools whereby other types of development could be analyzed (Bloom, 1964).

He then proceeds to discuss intelligence using the analytical tool developed from the discussion on height. Based on his studies, Bloom puts forth the view that there is definitely a correlation between intelligence at a certain age and intelligence at maturity, just as there was a correlation in height. Therefore, intelligence also may be regarded as a stable characteristic.

When intelligence was measured at age seventeen, it was shown that 20 percent of that intelligence was acquired by age one; 50 percent by age four; 80 percent by age eight; 92 percent by age thirteen; and the rest by age seventeen. This explains Bloom's stress on the right type of environment for young children since they develop most of their intelligence during their early years. He believes that the early years are extremely important for the following reasons: (1) Certain characteristics grow very rapidly during these early years, and the environment is important in that any variation shapes the formation of these characteristics; (2) According to developmentalists, the early years form the basis for later development and the accomplishment of the early development stages is helped by a conducive environment; (3) First learning takes place more easily than later learning, which might be interfered with by early learning. Therefore, it is important that the correct form of learning take place in early childhood aided by a meaningful environment (Bloom, 1964).

Many studies support Bloom's views on the importance of the early environment (Bloom, 1964). Bloom states that the developmental curve reaches midpoint before the age of five for certain characteristics. Thus the environment would have its greatest effect on a characteristic during the period of its most rapid development (Bloom, 1964).

Table IV

DEVELOPMENTAL CURVE

Height	Age 2½
General intelligence	Age 4
Aggressiveness in males*	Age 3
Dependence in females*	Age 4
Intellectuality in males and females*	Age 4
General school achievement	Grade 3

*Since we do not have an absolute scale for the characteristics, we have indicated the age at which one-half of the criterion variance can be predicted (Bloom, 1964, p. 205).

In describing learning experiences, Bloom mentions Ralph W. Tyler, in *Basic Principles of Curriculum and Instruction.* Tyler describes the learning experience as the interaction between the learner and the external conditions in the environment. Active behavior on the part of the student is necessary before learning takes place. He doesn't learn by having the teacher do things but rather *he* does, *he* learns.

BLOOM'S APPLICATION AND RESEARCH

Bloom's theory of learning stems from an educator's point of view. When he incorporated research with his theory of learning, he developed a classification of knowledge. In his book, *Taxonomy of Educational Objectives,* Bloom has divided all learning processes into three domains: (1) cognitive, (2) affective, (3) psychomotor. This taxonomy was developed out of a need to do a better job of evaluating learning and constructing tests, but it is an important consideration. Since our primary interest is in the cognitive domain, it is briefly outlined as follows:

"1.00 Knowledge — Knowledge, as defined here, involves the recall of specifics and universals, the recall of methods and processes, or the recall of a pattern, structure, or setting.

1.10 Knowledge of specifics — The recall of specific and isolated bits of information. The emphasis is on symbols with concrete referents.

1.30 Knowledge of the universals and abstractions in a field — Knowledge of the major schemes and patterns by which phenomena and ideas are organized.

2.00 Comprehension — This represents the lowest level of understanding. It refers to a type of understanding or apprehension in which the individual knows what is being communicated and can make use of the material or idea being communicated without necessarily relating it to other material or seeing its fullest implications.

2.10 Translation — Comprehension as evidenced by the care and accuracy with which the communication is paraphrased or rendered from one language or form of communication to another.

2.20 Interpretation — The explanation or summarization of a communication.

2.30 Extrapolation — The extension of trends or tendencies beyond the given data to determine implications, consequences, corollaries, effects, etc., which are in accordance with the conditions described in the original communications.

3.00 Application — The use of abstractions in particular and concrete situations. The abstractions may be in the form of general ideas, rules of procedures, or generalized methods.

4.00 Analysis — The breakdown of a communication into its constituent elements or parts such that the relative hierarchy of ideas is made clear and/or the relations between the ideas expressed are made explicit.

4.10 Analysis of elements — Identification of the elements included in a communication.

4.20 Analysis of relationships — The connections and interactions between elements and parts of a communication.

4.30 Analysis of organizational principles — The organization, systematic arrangement, and structure which hold the communication together.

5.00 Synthesis — The putting together of elements and parts so as to form a whole. This involves the process of working with pieces, parts, elements, etc., and arranging and combining them in such a way as to constitute a pattern or structure not clearly there before.

5.10 Production of a unique communication — The development of a communication in which the writer or speaker attempts to convey ideas, feelings, and/or experiences to others.

5.20 Production of a plan or proposed set of operations — The development of a plan of work or the proposal of a plan or operation. The plan should satisfy requirements of the task which may be given to the student or which he may develop for himself.

5.30 Derivation of a set of abstract relations — The

development of a set of abstract relations either to classify or /to/ explain particular data or phenomena, or the deduction of propositions and relations from a set of basic propositions or symbolic representations.

6.00 Evaluation — Judgments about the value of material and methods for given purposes. Quantitative and qualitative judgments about the extent to which material and methods satisfy criteria. Use of a standard appraisal.

6.10 Judgments in terms of internal evidence — Evaluation of the accuracy of a communication from such evidence as logical accuracy, consistency, and other internal criteria.

6.20 Judgments in terms of external criteria — Evaluation of material with reference to selected or remembered criteria." (Bloom, 1956)*

In the above outline of "knowledge," Bloom has classified types of learning in such a way that the teacher can aim a task at the specific area of skill in which the student needs to improve.

Learning is only complete when the goal is reached and when the principles are understood. Bloom emphasizes the early environment of a child as being very important to the development of that child's intelligence. He also stresses the fact that a good teacher should provide a variety of learning methods for the child to use.

BLOOM'S MASTERY LEARNING IN THE CLASSROOM

Bloom's work on the taxonomy of educational objectives led him to investigate and attempt to explain in-

---

*From *TAXONOMY OF EDUCATIONAL OBJECTIVES: The Classification of Educational Goals: HANDBOOK I: COGNITIVE DOMAIN* by Benjamin S. Bloom et al. Copyright © 1956 by Longman Inc. Reprinted by permission.

dividual differences in school learning and how these differences may be altered in the best interest of the student, the school, and society. His investigation culminated in his book *Human Characteristics and School Learning* in which he details his key concept of Mastery Learning. Mastery Learning is at the foundation of a learning theory that attempts to explain school learning in terms of a small number of variables. Mastery Learning says, in essence, that what any person in the world can learn, almost all persons can learn *if* provided with appropriate prior and current conditions of learning. Bloom believes that most of the individual differences in school learning may be regarded as man-made and accidental rather than fixed in the individual at the time of conception. He sees three interdependent variables as responsible for the vast majority of variation in learning:

A. The extent to which the student has already learned the basic prerequisites of the learning to be accomplished. (Cognitive Entry Behaviors — CEB).

B. The extent to which the student is (or can be) motivated to engage in the learning process. (Affective Entry Characteristics — AEC).

C. The extent to which the instruction to be given is appropriate to the learner. (Quality of Instruction — Q of I).

According to Bloom, differences in the CEB of students account for 50 percent of the learning variations in school. It is critical for the teacher to understand all prerequisite learning necessary for success in a given task, determine which students have/have not mastered those prerequisites, and make provision for such prerequisite learning if needed.

The learner's AEC can account for up to one-fourth of the variance of achievement on courses or learning tasks. These affective entry characteristics are largely determined by the individual's perception of his success or failure with previous learning tasks that he believes to be similar or related. It is very difficult for a learner to achieve mastery on a learning task if he has a negative AEC. Interestingly, AECs are primarily with in-school variables. That is, the student gains his perceptions about how well he is learning from feedback from the evidence and judgments of his teachers, parents, and peers. Thus the teacher plays a vital role in encouraging the development of positive affective characteristics toward school learning and self at every stage of the school process. The teacher's efforts to make each learning experience as enjoyable and successful for the student as possible will have tremendous influence upon the AEC. The student's chances of success are enhanced if the teacher provides for all the CEB needed and gives Quality Instruction.

In defining Quality of Instruction, Bloom describes four subvariables that appear to promote learning:

A. Cues — how the teacher makes clear to the student what is to be learned, what the student is to do, and how he is to do it. Techniques include explanation, illustration, demonstration, etc. The key is to adapt or alter the cues in the way that works best for the learner.

B. Participation — or practice of the responses to be learned. Again, the method and amount should be tailored to the needs of the student.

C. Reinforcement — (positive or negative) at various stages in the learning process. Adaptation to the learner and variation of type is important.

D. Feedback and Corrective Procedures — in Mastery Learning, students receive feedback on what they have learned and what they still need to learn to achieve the mastery criterion, plus they receive corrective instruction in which the cues, practice, and reinforcement are adapted to individual needs.

Bloom feels that the Q of I accounts for about one-fourth of the differences in learning in schools. It is vital that teachers be effective in all four subvariables of the Q of I.

Bloom's Theory is more concerned with the process of learning in school situations rather than with particular educational objectives, subject matter, etc. His major point is that a system of feedback to the teachers and students can reveal the errors in learning shortly after they occur, and if appropriate corrections are introduced as they are needed; the large majority (80%) of students in a class can learn selected subjects up to as high a level (85%) as the most able students in the group.

Chapter 4

LAWRENCE KOHLBERG

Lawrence Kohlberg was born in Bronxville, New York in 1929. He received the B.A. degree from the University of Chicago in 1948 and his Ph.D. degree in 1958. He was Assistant Professor of Psychology at Yale, 1959-61, fellow at the Center of Advanced Study of Behavioral Science, 1961-62, Assistant Professor of Psychology and Human Development at University of Chicago, 1962-64, Director of Center for Moral Education Harvard University. Kohlberg is the author of **Moral Development and Moral Education** *and* **The Development of Modes of Moral Thinking and Choice in the Years 10 to 16.**

MORAL development has been the subject of educators for centuries, so Kohlberg was not the originator of the cognitive-developmental approach to moral education. The first major proponent of this method was Socrates, who believed that a universal conception of justice was latent in everyone and was developed cognitively by stages through doubt, discussions, and questionings.

John Dewey recaptured this theory by proposing three levels of moral development: (1) premoral, (2) conventional, and (3) autonomous. Jean Piaget divided moral development into three levels, which he called (1) the premoral level (0-4 years), (2) the heteronomous level (4-8 years), and (3) the autonomous level (8-12 years) (Kohlberg, 1975). Kohlberg redefined and validated the Dewey-Piaget stages and organized them into three levels, each of which had two stages. They are as follows:

I. *Preconventional Level:* At this level, the child is responsive to cultural rules and labels of good and bad, right and wrong, but interprets these labels in terms either of the physical or the hedonistic consequences of action (punishment, reward, exchange of favors), or in terms of the physical power of those who enunciate the rules and labels. This level is divided into the following two stages:

Stage 1: The punishment and obedience orientation.

Stage 2: The instrumental-relativist orientation. Right actions consist of that which instrumentally satisfies one's own needs and occasionally the needs of others.

II. *Conventional Level:* At this level, maintaining the expectations of the individual's family, group, or nation is perceived as valuable in its own right, regardless of immediate and obvious consequences. The attitude is not only one of conformity to personal expectations and social order but of loyalty to it; of actively maintaining, supporting, and justifying the order; and of identifying with the persons or group involved in it. There are two stages at this level:

Stage 3: The interpersonal concordance or "good boy-nice girl" orientation. Good behavior is that which pleases or helps others and is approved by them.

Stage 4: Authority and social order maintaining orientation.

III. *Postconventional, Autonomous, or Principled Level:* At this level, there is a clear effort to define moral values and principles that have validity and application apart from the authority of the groups or persons holding these principles and apart from the individual's own identification with these groups. This level has the following two stages:

Stage 5: The social-contract legalistic orientation. Right action tends to be defined in terms of general individual rights and standards that have been critically examined and agreed upon by the whole society.

Stage 6: The universal-ethical principle orientation. Right is defined by the decision of conscience in accord with self-chosen ethical principles appealing to logical comprehensiveness, universality, and consistency. (Kohlberg, 1975)*

Kohlberg feels that the interaction between an individual and his peers as well as authority figures results in cognitive development, which in turn leads to growth from one stage to a higher stage. This interaction involves trying different roles and observing others, thus learning about rules, standards, and motivations. As an individual matures and participates in societal groups, his view of the social-moral world also changes accordingly (Klausmeier and Goodwin, 1975).

All individuals, according to Kohlberg, follow the same sequence regarding the stages of development, but all do not necessarily reach the last stage (Klausmeier and Goodwin, 1975). The stage of moral development in which an individual operates and his IQ or verbal intelligence have no significant correlation. However, the individual's level of cognitive development is important because it sets limits on the stage of moral development that can be attained. Though 50 percent of adults are

---

*From "The Cognitive-Developmental Approach to Moral Education" by Lawrence Kohlberg. © 1975 *Phi Delta Kappa.* Reprinted by permission.

capable of reasoning at the highest stage of moral development, only 10 percent are attaining the corresponding level of moral development (Kohlberg, 1975).

There are numerous age differences in individuals who have all reached the same stage of moral development. Also, overlapping of stages is found while an individual is in transition from one stage to the next one (Klausmeier and Goodwin, 1975).

These stages that have been discussed form the backbone of Kohlberg's approach to moral education. He offers a cognitive-developmental approach to the study of attitudes, values, and morals, which can be used to accelerate the level of moral reasoning in children and adults.

The interaction between an individual and significant others leads to cognitive development, the result of which is the graduation from one stage to the next.

PRACTICAL APPLICATION OF KOHLBERG

In their book *Promoting Moral Growth,* Hersh, Paolitto, and Reimer offer a plan for a Moral Development Curriculum based on Kohlberg's Theory. Their suggestions can be used by teachers and the basic principles adopted by parents. These authors suggest ten steps:

1. Develop a rationale — an understanding of Kohlberg's theoretical constructs is absolutely necessary. The rationale is a personal translation of the theory and is required for enhancing clarity in the curriculum-building process.

2. Identify moral issues in the curriculum — by examining curriculum materials, i.e. literature, history, art, for relationships among persons or between persons and institutions. Or, these issues may center on events in the

home, classroom, school, or society. One must assess the issues in relation to the level of reasoning and social role-taking perspective required of the students.

3. Relate the moral issues to students' lives — students should respond to such questions as, Have you ever faced this type of situation or conflict? What would (could, did, should) you do?

4. Use materials that promote role-taking — role-taking means taking another person's perspective. This helps clarify conflicting issues and makes moral questions more real. Moral development requires that a person realize that people are different with respect to attitudes, thoughts, abilities, feelings, and viewpoints. By role-taking, students move from a self-centered view of the world to where they can see themselves from an external perspective. Role-taking is critical to development because it enables people to experience moral viewpoints that conflict with their own. Cognitive conflict promotes the development of moral reasoning.

5. Expose students to more adequate reasoning structures — the structure of reasoning in the curriculum should be slightly higher than the reasoning level of the student. For most people, reasoning one stage above their own creates cognitive disequilibrium and initiates developing a new reasoning structure.

6. Encourage students to be curriculum developers — opportunities for students to ferret out any moral issues *they* find are essential. Once students become aware of moral issues, they will be quick to point them out.

7. Work with another colleague — often we find that another's thinking out loud jogs our own thinking; the result is greater than the sum of two separate individuals' thoughts. Teachers need support and dialogue even as students do. Being able to share doubts, questions, and

successes with a colleague will help create a supportive environment.

8. Do a pilot test of material — the use of mini-units may provide a good test of one's first efforts. By asking a colleague to observe and asking students for their reactions, necessary changes can be made. Were the issues too hypothetical or too real? Were the probing questions sufficient to cause disequilibrium?

9. Examine materials beyond textbook data — you can utilize movies, television, records, novels, poetry, art, and newspapers. Once their moral awareness is heightened, students will recognize moral issues everywhere. At this point, you will have to become more selective in your material.

10. Develop experiences in which students can act on their reasoning — the opportunity to *act* provides a test of reasoning. Other activities in school or personal life — clubs, athletics, student government — provide opportunities to transfer moral reasoning to moral action. It is crucial to encourage this behavior and provide time to discuss such events. Having students act on their reasoning is an important ingredient in helping them move from moral reasoning to moral behavior (Hersh, Paolitto, Reimer, 1979).*

*From *PROMOTING MORAL GROWTH: From Piaget to Kohlberg,* 1st edition, by Richard H. Hersh, Diana Pritchard Paolitto, and Joseph Reimer. Copyright © 1979 by Longman Inc. Reprinted by permission.

Chapter 5

ROBERT HAVIGHURST

Robert J. Havighurst is Professor of Education and Human Development at the University of Chicago. Professor Havighurst received his Ph.D. from Ohio State University. He has served as president of the Gerontological Society, Secretary of the Society for Research in Child Development, consultant to the Rockefeller Foundation and director of the Program for Youth and Educational Development in Central Europe. Dr. Havighurst has received many honors in his long and distinguished career and is well known for his books in the field of human development.

HAVIGHURST has identified developmental tasks that must be mastered if the child is to develop normally. Developmental tasks are tasks "which arise at or about a certain period in the life of the individual, successful achievement of which leads to happiness in the individual, disapproval by the society, and difficulty with later tasks" (Havighurst, 1953).

Havighurst identifies a sequential series of tasks that occur at every stage of development. These are sequential not only in the sense that progression is ordinarily continuous but also in the sense that one task is frequently a prerequisite for successful mastery of subsequent tasks. The mastery of each task is not only brought about by functional, maturational factors; it is also a function of personal efforts as well as the expectations of societal norms that are communicated to children.

Havighurst's developmental task theory is noteworthy for its "teachable moment" concept. According to this concept, there are situations that arise incidentally in the classroom, and these "moments" should be capitalized on as they are critical periods during which a particular task can be mastered most easily and that failure to do so at that time may lead to considerable difficulties in mastering tasks later. Efforts at teaching that may seem fruitless will yield gratifying results if undertaken at the teachable moment when mastery of the task has its best chance of succeeding. An example of the teachable moment could be taken from the area of speech where the critical period for acquiring language is between the age of twelve to eighteen months. Failure to acquire speech during this period could lead to emotional disturbances in the child and also some other maladjustments (Havighurst, 1953).

The human body has many possibilities for development. These possibilities depend on what the individual learns. Life itself is made up of a series of learning tasks. Happiness, satisfaction, and rewards are a result of the ability to learn well. Poor learning leads to unhappiness and disapproval by society (Havighurst, 1953).

Because the developmental tasks are sequential, one can see the importance attached to the acquisition of early tasks, especially since they are prerequisites for the successful mastery of later tasks. For this reason, the tasks of infancy and early childhood are extremely important, and they will be discussed in this paper.

According to Havighurst (1953), the tasks are as follows:

1. *Learning to walk.* The basic skills required for walking are readily mastered between the ages of nine and fifteen months. Later skills such as running, skipping, and jumping are dependent on this early mastery.

2. *Learning to take solid foods.* The child is biologically and physiologically ready to handle solid foods during the

second year of life. The feeding schedule and the method and age of weaning have lasting effects upon his personality.

3. *Learning to talk.* The ability to make meaningful sounds that serve as a source of communication with other people is acquired between the ages of twelve and eighteen months. As has been mentioned before, the child is apt to become emotionally disturbed if he fails to acquire the skills of speech at this time.

4. *Learning to control the elimination of body wastes.* This task consists of learning to urinate and defecate according to acceptable societal norms. This is mastered between the ages of two and four years.

5. *Learning sex differences and sexual modesty.* Very early in his life, the child is made aware of sex differences. He is taught that boys and girls have to conform to accepted forms of behavior that are sex based. He is made aware of and taught how to deal with anatomical differences. The attitudes and feelings that he develops toward sex and sexual behavior during these early years most likely will have a lasting effect upon his sexuality throughout life.

6. *Achieving physiological stability.* This is achieved by the time the child is five years old and is the only biological task of the series. A stable organism is conducive to successful achievement in other areas.

7. *Forming simple concepts of social and physical reality.* Amidst the confusion surrounding him, the child discovers order and regularity and thus makes generalizations. Certain people take care of his needs and look after him. He develops auditory and visual perceptions — he can distinguish among different sounds, shapes, types. His nervous system has developed to a certain level making the understanding of these concepts possible. What he needs now is enough stimulation and experiences in order

for him to form more concepts and understand them properly. His later mental development is dependent on his ability to function at this level now.

8. *Learning to relate oneself emotionally to parents, siblings, and others.* Through gestures and language, the young child shares his experiences with others. He imitates the behavior of significant others and participates in role-playing. He also learns to identify with others, particularly with his parents. The method whereby he relates emotionally to others helps determine his personality type and its bearing on his social relations in later life.

9. *Learning to distinguish right and wrong and developing a conscience.* The concepts of good and bad need to be learned and based on an internalized value structure, not on the consequences of certain forms of behavior, i.e. pleasure is good, pain is evil. His parents' values and their actions that are based on these values help form his conscience upon which his moral character and ethical values will be based.

RESEARCH. The critical periods theory has been supported in various ways by Von Senden, Lorenz, Sitz, and Piaget. These periods or stages may exist in the development of fundamental sensory processes such as perceptual abilities and in the development of social behavior as well. According to this theory, these stages are of limited duration. There may be definite periods during which certain tasks have to be mastered if they are to become part of individuals' repertoire of responses. There also may be periods of peak efficiency for the acquisition of an experience before which it cannot be acquired and after which the level of receptivity remains constant.

From the above, it becomes apparent that developmental tasks may arise from (a) the values, aspirations, and desires of the emerging personality, (b) the pressure of cultural processes upon the individual, or (c) physical maturation. They arise in most cases from combinations of these factors acting together.

Havighurst's developmental tasks are very thorough in their descriptions of what occurs during the various physiological, psychological, and cultural stages of development. While keeping these stages in mind, it is apparent that parents, teachers, and other significant adults in a child's life must bear in mind that as children, each individual progresses at his own rate during the various stages of tasks. Certainly, this factor alone should make those "significant" adults more perceptive and receptive to the individual needs of the child.

Children should be considered from the physiological, psychological, and cultural viewpoints. By considering these factors, programs may be designed that will enable the child to develop in the best possible way.

Mastery of the basic skills in childhood is necessary for a happy and successful adult life.

HAVIGHURST — PRACTICAL APPLICATION

Havighurst's next age group is called middle childhood and covers the period from approximately six to twelve years of age. This age is characterized by three great outward pushes: the thrust of the child out of the home and into the peer group; the physical thrust into the world of games and work requiring neuromuscular skills; the mental thrust into the world of adult concepts, logic, symbolism, and communication. During this period, the child encounters developmental tasks that have implications for both teacher and parents. These tasks and their educational implication are

A. Learning Physical Skills Necessary for Ordinary

Games — Teachers and parents should be particularly aware of children who have difficulty in this area and provide physical training to alleviate or modify the problem.

B. Building Wholesome Attitudes Toward Oneself as a Growing Organism — Health habits should be taught routinely. Sex education should be a matter of agreement between the school and parents with the school doing what the parents feel they cannot do so well. Teachers should be on the watch for troubled, confused children and should arrange for individual counseling.

C. Learning to Get Along With Age-Mates — Often, the key to understanding a child's difficulties with his school subjects or to understanding a discipline problem in class is given by a knowledge of his difficulties in achieving this particular developmental task. The skillful teacher studies and understands the peer culture of the school and community. She uses sociometric devices to learn the social structure of her particular class. She learns to both cooperate with the peer group in some of its activities and direct and control it as places where it may do harm to individual children.

D. Learning an Appropriate Masculine or Feminine Social Role — The sex role is taught by so many other agencies that teachers probably have little more than a remedial function and to serve as a proper model. It is generally agreed that more male teachers for children of this age would have a good influence on boys.

E. Developing Fundamental Skills in Reading, Writing, and Calculating — Developmental psychology and learning theory suggest that less pressure be put on children to learn to read and write at the age of six or seven. Pressure to succeed in these skills before the child is biologically, psychologically, or mentally ready can create long-term learning disabilities as well as self-concept problems. Usually, children learn these skills very rapidly and easily if allowed to wait until a year or two later.

F. Developing Concepts Necessary for Everyday Living — Both parents and teachers should provide as many concrete experiences dealing with daily life. Concepts about diet, disease, health, agriculture, et cetera, can be taught by direct hands-on experience and activity in connection with school lunch, gardens, and local health programs. The early inclusion of such subjects as history, geography, and even math is questionable considering the child's limited concepts of time, space, and number.

G. Developing Conscience, Morality, and a Scale of Values — The school affects the child's conscience and his morality:

1. through its teachings about morality
2. through the teacher's punishments and rewards
3. through the teacher's examples, and
4. through the child's experience with his peer group.

H. Achieving Personal Independence — If teachers hope to promote the personal independence of their students, they will teach them how to study, work, and learn independently; give them opportunity to plan a part of the school program and discuss or criticize the results of their planning; provide the kind of supervision that supports children when they make mistakes and sets limits for their growing independence to protect them from going too far.

I. Developing Attitudes Toward Social Groups and Institutions — Schools and teachers should work to inculcate the basic social attitudes that are generally agreed upon as desirable for all Americans. For example, attitudes of religious and racial tolerance, respect for freedom of speech and other civil rights, political democracy, and international cooperation.

Havighurst has several other groups of developmental tasks for later age groups but these are beyond the scope of this book.

Chapter 6

MARIA MONTESSORI

Maria Montessori was born in 1870 and died 1952. She was the first woman ever granted a medical degree by an Italian university. She worked in the fields of psychiatry, hygiene, pedagogy, and anthropology. An ardent feminist, she revolutionized modern thinking about children and their education throughout the world. Working with handicapped children, she developed materials and methods with which they were able to perform school problems previously considered far beyond their capacity. She then moved on to work with normal children of the slums. Thereafter by her own desire and by public demand, she was an educator, not a medical doctor. Dr. Montessori's insights and methods are contained in four basic texts: **The Montessori Method; Spontaneous Activity in Education; The Montessori Elementary Material;** *and* **Dr. Montessori's Own Handbook.**

MONTESSORI believed that education is a process that begins at birth and that the first few years of life, the formative years, are the most important for the child's cognitive development. For a baby to develop into a normal, well-rounded individual, he must have contact with other people. He must be picked up, cuddled, and given a lot of attention. The baby's active mind needs stimulation, a necessary ingredient for development. The child will become apathetic if he is constantly isolated. Behavior patterns and adult thought patterns are brought about through normal, gradual processes of learning. The learning methods used during the first six years of life will largely determine what type of adult the child will turn out to be. The early years are important and should be taken advantage of, because it is during these years that the rate of growth of the mental processes is extremely rapid (Hainstock, 1968).

Montessori's pedagogical ideas were not broad enough to encompass her view of the role of the child. Adult attitudes toward children needed to be reformulated. They needed to realize that if the child were allowed to utilize his hidden talents and potentialities, he would be transformed. This transformation would carry over into adulthood where the individual would make meaningful contributions to society. Montessori felt that education was too preoccupied with producing results rather than producing well-rounded individuals. She saw the child as playing an important part in his own development. What he would become depended on how much freedom adults allowed him to develop his true self. "She questioned the efficacy, in its then present form, of the main, though not only instrument of education — the school" (Rambush, 1962).

For Montessori, there is just normal human development with its basis in cognition, since she maintains that man is a rational animal. With the development of reason along normal lines and the increase of cognitive powers, the child will develop certain views about the world, others, and more importantly, about himself. He will be independent, not servile. He will not try to control other people's actions, nor will he let them control his. He will use reason, not threats and intimidation, when dealing with others. His relationship with others thus depends on his level of personal independence (Berliner, 1974).

Considered to be radically ahead of her time in the early 1900s, when she advocated early cognitive learning,

Montessori's ideas today constitute the framework for many of our modern educational practices. She recognized that the best years are those from birth to six, when behavior patterns and adult thought processes were established. Montessori had great respect for the young child and felt that his great potential had not been challenged sufficiently.

Through her observation of children, Montessori developed her method, which she termed the "discovery of the child." She approached it in a scientific way, the aim being, through motor, sensory, and intellectual activities, to develop the whole personality of the child.

Montessori's deep insights and teaching methods can infuse new life into education, especially when too little emphasis is placed on a well-rounded preschool education. It has exposed children to learning earlier in life and will help them to become intelligent, thinking adults (Hainstock, 1968).

Dr. Montessori developed a curriculum that included the following ideas:

ENVIRONMENT: She felt that the child should not be pressured to learn. Given a conducive learning environment, he would be free to develop at his own rate. "Thus Montessori felt there must be freedom within the prepared environment to develop his physical, mental, and spiritual growth" (Hainstock, 1968). Since the child acquires a large amount of knowledge during the first six years of life, Montessori has developed a special environment for him where he can move around at will, working, touching things, and absorbing what he finds. He learns a lot through hands-on experience. His intellect starts working when he moves, thus learning materials are geared towards the child's learning through movement. By following successive steps, during which the five senses are developed and refined, the child is readied for the more formal types of learning (Kocher, 1973).

The aim of a structured environment is to lead the child towards independence. His physical needs determine the structure of the environment. This means adapting furnishings, windows, toilets, et cetera, to a child's size. Coupled with the structure, an important thing to remember is that the environment should be neat and orderly.

DIRECTRESS. Parents play an important role in the child's development. They are the child's first teachers. They help the child explore the world around him. Being parents, they can discover the child's attitudes, strengths, and weaknesses. They can help the child develop healthy attitudes towards learning so that when he enters school, he is well prepared and has a good self-concept (Drem, 1974).

The environment would be useless to the child unless he has someone to act as a link between himself and this structured environment. This link is teacher: the directress (or director) who introduces the child to an activity, lets him develop by using it, and helps him where necessary. She also monitors his progress carefully. "Her ideal is that the child should increasingly become the more active partner in the environment and herself the more passive" (Kocher, 1973).

Montessori said that "the thing we should cultivate in our teachers is more the spirit than the mechanical skill of the scientist" (Hainstock, 1968). The child should be allowed to teach himself. The teacher serves as a guide, leading the child into new learning experiences, introducing enough variety in order that he remains enthusiastic. The child wants to express his individuality by selecting tasks to accomplish. He follows tasks through to completion, modifying them where necessary to suit his needs. The teacher should thus learn to respect the child and realize that he is entitled to his privacy. Children learn from role-models, therefore, teachers should be the best models possible. They possess a strong willingness to learn and are eager to please, but they need encouragement and praise.

MATERIALS. The teachers should guide the child, not take him by the hand and lead him. Thus, when introducing new learning materials, directions should be minimal, but clearly understood. Only then should the child work with the materials. Materials should be introduced gradually, and progressively, with the emphasis being on *child* discovery, the teacher's role being more a passive one (Hainstock, 1968).

Sensorial exercises play an important part in this learning process. Their goal is to develop the child's intellect and control to the point where the child is ready for more advanced work. Sensory exercises would include visual, auditory, tactile, thermal, basic kinesthetic, olifactory, awareness, shapes, dimensional, and quantity experiences (Hainstock, 1968).

Montessori's method is characterized by a large measure of individual initiative and self-direction. The main goals today seem to be the teaching of skills and the transfer of knowledge. Montessori is designed to help the child build within himself the foundation for a lifetime. With this method, a balanced development can take place and a personality that is strong enough to cope with our rapidly changing world can be formed.

Chapter 7

JEAN PIAGET

Jean Piaget is often compared to Sigmund Freud in the scope of his influence on psychology. Born on August 9, 1896, in Neuchâtel, Switzerland, he was a child prodigy who published important papers on molluscs while he was in high school. Piaget received his doctoral degree in natural science at the University of Neuchâtel in 1918. Three years later, he received a second doctorate in logic and philosophy, became a professor there in 1926, professor of psychology at the University of Geneva in 1929, and professor of general psychology at Lausanne University in Italy in 1937. His life-work was centered on investigating how children form concepts of space, time, velocity, force, and chance. Piaget is the author of more than a hundred articles and over forty books. Among them are **Origins of Intelligence in Children** *and* **The Construction of Reality in the Child.** *Piaget served as director of the International Center for Genetic Epistemology. Piaget has had more influence upon the field of cognitive development than any other person of the century.*

MODERN psychologists and educators have all displayed interest in the work of Piaget. He has brought a new dimension to the study of child development with his theories on thought development of the child problems that hindered the mental evolution. Because of his theories, current ideas on child development have had to be adjusted. Certain experts feel that his theories offer a viable alternative to the stimulus-response behaviorist tradition. Above all, Piaget's theory of

45

child development, as opposed to other theories, is "the one most securely founded upon the study of the child" (Ginsburg and Opper, 1969).

As a pioneer in this field, Piaget could view intelligence according to his perspective. The main thrust of his work was to find out how intelligence was structured. As a result of this thrust, it is not too difficult to see why he is mainly interested in mental activity. This mental activity takes place as the individual interacts with his environment. The child learns, not as an observer, but through active involvement.

Through study, Piaget viewed intelligence as involving biological adaptation, gradual evolution, equilibrium between the individual and the environment, and mental activity. These do not include the possibility of individual differences in intelligence. Piaget is aware of these differences, but he does not dwell on them. What he seeks to do is to abstract from all these differences one general description of thought.

Average levels of cognitive functioning are not included in Piaget's theories. They deal instead with the highest levels of thought possible at a given stage. "In essence, Piaget looks at intelligence in terms of content, structure, and function" (Ginsburg and Opper, 1969).

Piaget's Theory

Piaget describes cognitive development in terms of a series of successive, overlapping stages that summarize major changes that take place in the thinking of normal children. His description is based on four concepts:

ASSIMILATION. This is the absorption of information by the brain; thus thinking includes incoming stimulation as well as the information already stored in the brain.

ACCOMODATION. As the brain absorbs new stimuli, thinking processes are changed to accommodate the new experiences.

SCHEMA. This is a structural unit of cognitive activity. It makes up the existing framework into which sensory data are fit, but that changes as assimilation and accommodation take place.

EQUILIBRATION. This is the process whereby schemata change from one stage to another.

Based on these concepts, Piaget describes changes in cognitive development in terms of four identifiable stages: sensori-motor, preoperational, concrete operational, and formal operational (Piaget, 1952).

The importance of internal processes in development and biological maturation of cognitive structures is given particular emphasis in Piaget's theory. It also assumes that there is no variation in the order of stages.

As the child acts upon his environment, intellectual growth occurs. Cognitive growth develops as assimilation, accommodation, and equilibration take place. Reorganization of the cognitive structure is constantly occurring as new ideas are assimilated and old ideas are accommodated. Most of Piaget's work is concerned with structural change.

The idea of equilibrium is important to this theory. It involves the relationship between assimilation and accommodation. The subject is constantly accommodating his schema as he assimilates new stimuli.

At all levels, cognitive behavior is a matter of subjective actions performed on reality. These actions became increasingly internalized and covert. The Piagetian concept connects action with thoughts. Logic can be used to describe motor activity. Thinking is regarded as essentially interiorized action (Piaget, 1952).

Piaget's stages of development follow a progression that suggests a fundamental continuity between physical and mental functioning. These stages will now be discussed.

Sensorimotor Period (birth to 2 years)

In this period, thinking is activated visually. Children understand only in terms of their sensations to what they see and in terms of their activities toward those visual stimuli. This is precisely why the world of infants is a world of the here and now; it is impossible for infants to sense an object or react to it when it is not physically present.

One of the major developmental achievements of this period is the eventual realization that objects continue to exist even when they are not immediately being sensed. This realization, sometimes referred to as the development of the *object concept,* is made possible by children's internalization of aspects of their environment. Internal representation makes thought possible. It also contributes significantly to the development of language because a word is an internalized representation of an object or activity.

There are six subdevelopmental stages during this period when the child changes from a *reflexive* to a *reflective* person:

1. Reflexive: behavior is elicited by certain stimuli
2. First Acquired Adaptation: action centers around the child's own body
3. Secondary Circular Reaction: by accident, a child produces a pleasurable effect and then attempts to replicate it
4. Clearer distinction between means and ends

5. Tertiary Circular Reactions: child varies a response
6. Invention of new means by mental combination of schemata.

The child's thinking at this period tends also to be "animistic," that is, the child ascribes life to inaminate objects that move (for example, seeing clouds as being self-propelled). This period ends when internal imagery and language begin.

Preoperational Period (2 to 7 years)

An operation is a mental activity or a thought that is subject to certain rules of logic, the most important of which is reversibility. A thought (internalized action) is reversible when it is capable of being "unthought." This means that the action it represents is capable of being reversed and the logical implications of doing so are understood. Because preoperational children cannot yet deal with operations, their thought processes are still irreversible.

Children's thoughts are dominated largely by their perceptions. Where there is an apparent conflict with perception and thought, they will rely on what they perceive rather than what they think. In addition, their solutions for many problems continue to be intuitive rather than logical. Some obstacles to logical thought include egocentrism, transformation, centration (center perception on a limited part of the stimulus), and reversibility (this is the most clearly defined aspect of logical thought according to Piaget).

Preoperational thought is transductive, that is, reasoning is from particular to particular.

At this period, the child cannot discover concepts,

though he can be taught concepts. He is egocentric — living in a private world. He cannot see that there are viewpoints different from his own; in fact, he is not even aware that other viewpoints exist.

Language development is the most important achievement during the preoperational period.

Concrete Operational Period (7 to 11 years)

The child attains the ability to conserve — ability to understand that the amount of something stays the same regardless of the changes in its shape or number of pieces into which it may be divided. The realization of conservation is important because it provides evidence of several logical rules that now govern the child's thinking. The most important logical rule is reversibility — the ability to reverse a process; in addition, children now understand identity and compensation. Thought for the first time becomes logical, though only for things that are concrete. The child has now acquired new abilities with respect to classes, seriation, and numbers.

Formal Operational Period (11 to 14 years)

Adult thinking is capable of taking place during this period, but any of the characteristics of the previous stages may surface. The ability to extrapolate is evident, and abstract thought is now possible. The child is very idealistic during this time. His thinking is characterized by scientific reasoning coupled with hypothesis testing. The thinking of adolescents is considered as propositional rather than concrete. A proposition is simply a statement that can be either right or wrong. It can be tied to the probable or improbable hypothetical or to objective reality.

The development of intelligence depends upon the direction in which intelligence evolves from simple reflexes to novel responses; the novelty is only in organization, not in components. According to Piaget, overt action and inner thinking can be characterized in the same general way and on the same general continuum.

Piaget believes that "background and environment will to a large extent determine the pace at which the child learns. All children, regardless of pace, must pass through the same phases of understanding. Skipping or reversing those phases poses a risk to the child's development. Unless children are given a continuing chance to use and test their developing abilities, their intellectual growth will be stunted" (Hechinger, 1972).

PRACTICAL APPLICATION OF PIAGET'S LEARNING THEORY

Piaget was more concerned with his theory of cognitive development than with its practical application for parents and teachers. And while he did develop certain tests and experiments to determine a child's cognitive state, it has been left largely to others to give specific guidance in the area of methodology. The following activities are recommended for parents/teachers who accept Piaget's theory.

A. Symbol-Picture-Logic-example —

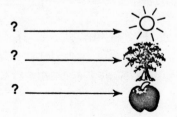

Directions — substitute something in place of the ? (answers S, T, A) The explicit meanings of the symbolic expressions are not verbalized. The children discover the exact logical meaning by repeated demonstration and by setting specific problems according to individual need. The equations are lengthened by the inclusion of such properties as addition, negation, conjunction, et cetera.

B. Probability Games — parent/teacher places eight red marbles and two yellow marbles in a bag and shakes it well. The bag is passed from one child to the other. Each must guess the color he will draw. After a marble is taken out and its color noted, it is put back in the bag.

C. Recognizing by touch — all that is needed is a box and two identical collections of small objects, with one collection displayed on a table, the other concealed in the box. The point of the game is to have the children look at a single object in one collection and find the identical object by touch alone in the other collection. Many variations can be developed.

D. Spatial Relations — there are many kinds of these games but they all boil down to knowing the location of certain points in space relative to other points. Reversals and sequencing are variations of this type of activity.

E. Communication — these activities involve at least two children. One child may have a set of multishaped objects in a specific design. He must communicate to the other child how to build a matching design. The task can be varied in many ways.

F. Sorting and Classifying — these kinds of activities are valuable in the practical application of Piaget's developmental theory.

G. Reality Acting — in which a child or group of children act out a real life experience. In reality acting, children do not merely play at thinking but are seriously engaged in thinking. They give reality to objects and situations.

H. Other General Activities — other beneficial activities include socio-dramatic play, art, block building, music, stories, and raising animals.

In this book *Piaget for the Classroom Teacher,* Wadsworth enumerates six principles of teaching based on Piagetian theory:

A. "Create an environment and atmosphere in which children will be active and initiate and complete their own activities. Provide time to spare and materials to complete self-initiated activities." To the extent possible, there should be no formal periods or time blocks. Children should be permitted to complete the activities they start and maintain interest in the activity even if interest is maintained for several days or longer.

B. "With regard to social-arbitrary knowledge, tell the child the right answer (give him feedback about his answers) and reinforces social-arbitrary knowledge. In physical knowledge, encourage the child to find the answer directly from activity or objects. In logical-mathematical knowledge, refrain from telling the right answer and reinforcing it."

1. Social-arbitrary knowledge specific to a culture, knowledge that is made by people, e.g. values. Reinforcement is desirable because the only source of social-arbitrary knowledge is other people.
2. Physical and logical-mathematical knowledge are based on the constructions of the child, and reinforcement here is undesirable. The child's "comprehension" is best if based on his constructions, not on the verbal information he receives.

C. "Let the preoperational child go through stages of

being 'wrong.' " In a sense, the young child's concepts are usually always "wrong." Their concepts are never quite fully developed. Before the development of formal operation, children are naturally and necessarily going to make mistakes.

D. "Some types of knowledge are best learned (and motivated) from interaction with other children." Where logical-mathematical thought and social-arbitrary thought are concerned, the peer group becomes an increasingly important factor:

1. in disequilibrating or shaking up the egocentric conceptualizations of the child and
2. in providing information or feedback to the child about the validity of his social and logical constructions.

E. "View all aspects of knowledge as inseparable." In the mind and actions of the child, knowledge exists as an inseparable whole.

F. "If you want a child to acquire a specific fact or piece of content that is not available to him, teach it directly and reinforce the learning." Care must be taken, however, not to confuse behavior with development or reinforcement-produced learning with development learning. Behaviors acquired as a consequence of reinforcement or punishment do not affect the development of the mind per se (Wadsworth, 1978).

Chapter 8

BURTON WHITE

Burton White is both Project Director and Principal Investigator for the Preschool Project of Harvard University's School of Education. He is the author of two major textbooks in the field of early childhood development and has written innumerable scholarly papers and contributions to symposia. Dr. White's work has been the subject of many magazine articles and eight television documentary films.

WHITE'S philosophy is based on the writings of Piaget on the origins of intelligence and Konrad Lorenz on ethology. He has accumulated knowledge on what children from birth to age six are like, what makes a fully developed, competent child, and how to provide experience that would be most beneficial to a child (White, 1975a).

White defines a fully developed or competent child as one who is "capable of coping with life's many aspects in a truly effective manner. This involves the adaptability or flexibility of functioning well in a variety of living conditions" (White, 1975a).

He evaluated compensatory preschool programs such as Head Start and came to the conclusion that these programs had not resulted in stopping or remedying the underachievement of poorly developed or disadvantaged three-to-five-year-old children.

According to White, patterns of low and high achievement can be observed by the age of two. He feels that the most important age span is from eight months to three years (White, 1975b). In this period, education in the form of informal schooling takes place primarily in the home. Since many children experience failure during this early schooling period, a pattern of failure is set that can continue throughout their lives (White, 1972). Thus White feels that the first three years should be our highest priority regarding education (White, 1975).

White (1973b, 1975b) identified four key processes in the child's development during the first three years of life:

1. *Language development.* Language skills, i.e. the use and understanding of it, are acquired when a child is six to eight months to about thirty-six months of age.

2. *Social attachment, style, and basic self-perceptions.* Early self-concept formation, development of social relationships, and adopting a unique social style are established in the first three years of life and are important for the child's future educational success.

3. *Curiosity.* The desire to explore the world and learn new things is well developed by the age of eight months. By the time the child reaches the age of two or three, this curiosity may have been crushed by improper child-rearing practices.

4. *Learning to learn skills.* If a child has not had the adequate motivation and stimulation necessary for proper development during the first few months of life, he will fall behind in this area midway in the second year of life.

From the above, one can see how important the first three years of life are in the child's development. "How these four processes fare as a consequence of child rearing practices seems to us to be fundamental in the development of each child" (White, 1975b).

White has not tried to explain how learning takes place, but rather he has determined factors in the environment that have been present in the early childhood experiences of a well-developed child. He feels that prevention is the best cure for learning problems.

White believes "that the requirements for adequate human development are modest during the first seven to nine months of life; so modest as to be available even in the poorest homes. The picture changes, however, when children become able to crawl about and to begin to process language" (White, 1975b). The first three years of the child's life are of crucial importance, and the attitudes of parents and the experiences that the child has largely determine his success or failure in school and life. White, therefore, believes parents need training in the early growth of children. His primary goal is to train parents in early child education so each family can do the best job they are capable of doing in raising "competent" children for society (White, 1973). These will be children who can achieve and feel confident and good about themselves and others.

IMPLICATIONS FOR TEACHERS

In a long-term study, White sought to discover what kinds of experiences, if any, are regularly associated with competence and incompetence development and identify the environmental inputs to those experiential differences. His research has convinced him that only a small minority of children develop as well as they could from eight months on. White describes major stress factors during the child's first few years of life and the effect of how these stresses are handled by the parents upon the development of competence in the child.

Such stresses involve the roaming, crawling, exploring eight or nine month old who sees the living room as being filled with exciting, novel, and perplexing scenes, where an adult sees only the same old stuff. This fascinating new world is not safe for the infant however. It is an easy place to create disorder, spill things, break valuable objects, et cetera. All of these factors stress the caretaker. In older children, ten to fourteen months, standing, walking, and climbing present even more dangerous possibilities, creating even greater stress on the mother/caretaker.

The fourteen to sixteen month old often (and quite normally) refuses to cooperate with his mother just for the sake of refusing. He is contesting her will and demonstrating his. To the inexperienced, unprepared mother, this first half of the second year can be very trying.

Without doubt, the source of stress most difficult to deal with is from the behavior of a not-much-older sibling. When children are spaced less than three years apart, families pay a significant price.

As a result of his research and in consideration of the stresses of the early childhood period, White concludes that there are three primary functions for caretakers of infants: designer, consultant, and authority. The following is a summary and description of how the more effective parents/caretakers handled these functions:

A. Designer (of the living area) — They protected the child from the dangers of the home (safety-proofing), *and* they protected the home from the child (child-proofing), usually ahead of time. They then provided maximum access to the living quarters. They particularly made the kitchen safe and useful. They made kitchen cabinets and safe utensils, et cetera, available for play.

B. Consulting — They were available to the child several hours daily to assist, enthuse, and soothe

when necessary. They usually responded prompt-
ly. They would pause to consider the baby's *purpose
of the moment*. They provided what was needed *with*
some language, on target and at or slightly above
his level of comprehension. They would add a
related idea or two and they would not prolong the
exchange longer than the baby wanted.

C. Authority — Though loving and encouraging and
free with praise, these mothers were firm. *No matter
how young the infant, they set clear limits*. They spoke a
disciplinary language the baby could understand.
They did not overintellectualize or expect the baby
to do more than he was capable of, like controlling
strong impulses indefinitely, et cetera.

All of White's findings certainly have practical importance for the caretakers of young children.

Chapter 9

TERREL H. BELL

Terrel H. Bell served as the U.S. Commissioner of Education for two years and is currently the Commissioner of Higher Education and Chief Executive Officer of the Board of Regents for the state of Utah. He has also served as Superintendent of Public Instruction in Utah and as Professor of School Administration at Utah State University. Dr. Bell was a member of the National Council on Educational Research and the National Council on Educational Statistics. Among his books are **Your Child's Intellect** *and* **A Performance Accountability System for School Administration.**

T. H. BELL, while U.S. Commissioner of Education, observed that the most successful schools in the nation were those where parents were actively involved in their child's school activities and where the schools reached out and included the parents in the child's educational planning. Through his work as a university professor, teacher, superintendent of schools, state school officer, and U.S. Commissioner of Education, he has come to believe that active parent stimulation of learning plays an important part in the child's later academic development.

Bell is an advocate of early childhood education in the home. He believes that preschool education should be given at home by the parents and not in an institutionalized setting. It is never too early to start this education. In fact, it should start at birth. The goal of this early education should be the creation of healthy attitudes about learning and the building of an intellectual capacity in preparation for formalized education.

The parents should be the child's first teachers. Parental love is the great strength of this early childhood education in the home. "Only this element — so essential to all babies and small children — can be provided in full measure by parents" (Bell, 1973). By using loving encouragement, not pressure and demands, learning will take place normally and naturally. Thus parents should be taught the fundamentals of early childhood education. A process of learning should be created in the home that would facilitate the intellectual growth of the child during the vital first five years of life.

Bell, commenting about parents who might feel that this home-based education would place excessive demands on their time, states that most of the tasks that develop cognitive growth in the child can be carried out as the parents do their daily duties around the house (Bell, 1973). Bell's approach to early childhood education assumes that children learn while playing, eating, dressing, helping around the house, and participating in regular family activities (Bell, 1973).

As parents employ the reinforcement theory and observe their children's development, they will get to know the strengths and weaknesses of their children. Daily, they will draw closer to their children, and this will help the children develop healthy self-concepts.

Parents should seize any opportunity for teaching their child. The techniques should be unstructured, "the teaching incidental and related to the real life experiences of parents and child" (Bell, 1973). No additional time is required of the parents. What is required, though, is a more educationally productive use of the time usually spent by parents with their children.

Bell gives general instructions and cautions. First, don't pressure the child to learn. A knowledge of development task periods would help parents know what and when to teach the child. Wait until he has matured enough to accomplish a particular task. Second, he recommends that parents adapt to the child's "peaks and valleys in learning" (Bell, 1973). Teach when the child's level of interest is high; stop when his interest is low. Pay careful notice to his attention span. Parents should also enjoy the teaching-learning situation.

Bell believes that the reinforcement theory is very important in this learning situation. Parents should use reinforcement to the child's benefit (reward appropriate behavior and extinguish that which is inappropriate).

The level of difficulty at which the child is working should be adjusted so that he responds correctly 80 percent of the time in a given learning situation. This includes the experience of reinforcement, while minimizing the number of incorrect responses. Thus the child feels success rather than failure.

In this home-based early childhood education program, household items and toys having educational value are used as teaching aids. These educational toys can be obtained from a number of libraries around the country. If these libraries are not available, parents should purchase the toys individually or in cooperation with other parents in their neighborhood. However, if none of these alternatives are viable, parents should utilize common household objects.

CRIB TOYS. These are toys for very young infants that are designed to stimulate sensory perceptions from the age of four months until the infant is ready to start crawling. These should be colorful as well as audible in order to stimulate the visual and listening capabilities. They should be attractive enough to the child so that he wants to reach for them, thus providing practice in limb coordination. They should capture the child's curiosity and should be changed often so as to provide for a variety of stimuli.

Toys for the Creeper (Crawler). At this stage, the child has acquired the ability to imitate, focus his eyes, grasp, reach, listen, and respond to various kinds of stimuli. The toys used now should match his perceptual abilities. Toys that develop listening, sight, and motor activities are recommended.

Toys That Teach Colors, Numbers, and the Alphabet. Toys in this group teach the identification of colors, numbers and number concepts, and also the letters of the alphabet. While being fun to play, these games also enable the child to master these concepts.

Toys That Teach Sight, Sound, and Touch Discrimination. These toys help sharpen the senses that need to be developed to the point where the child is ready to use them upon entering school. They would include pictures, shapes, and exercises to develop the haptic sense.

The goals to be achieved by the use of these materials are the development of the child's latent mental powers to the fullest and the ability to enjoy learning and develop healthy attitudes toward this learning.

These materials help parents reach these goals. These toys are challenging, require the use of the senses individually or in combination, and involve both mental and physical activity. Since most toys require two or more persons to play the games, the parent is usually directly involved. These toys have a specific purpose and should be put away when not in use. They should be regarded as special and their use eagerly anticipated by the child.

What distinguishes educational toys from ordinary toys is the fact that they are designed to teach certain concepts and build some skills, whereas ordinary toys are primarily used for recreation and amusement. Educational toys have been developed by various companies who have tested them with children in actual learning-playing situations. The instructions to these games have been written from the evaluation of the results. Bell also has prepared a program of preschool home education that includes materials, techniques, and recommendations for the child's first five years of life.

The above program is Bell's approach to home-based early childhood education, which teaches according to an unstructured format. The rationale behind this approach is that the child's learning ability will increase as he watches and listens to his parents and his environment in everyday activities. It is out of these activities that teaching opportunities arise as a result of the interaction between parents and child. Certain educational toys could be used to aid the parent in creating a continually challenging and stimulating environment that will facilitate the child's cognitive growth, thus preparing him for later, structured educational activities.

Chapter 10

SUMMARY AND CONCLUSION

W E have seen how children learn, according to various experts. We discussed Bruner's three stages of (1) action, (2) imagery, and (3) symbolism and the theory that a child could learn anything if he was led through these stages. Bloom and Montessori emphasized the importance of the early environment in the development of the child's intelligence. Montessori also believed that the child learns through individual initiative and self-direction and, along with Bloom, stressed that teachers should help structure the environment by providing a variety of learning materials and methods.

Havighurst's developmental stages, along with its "teachable moment" concept, and Piaget's stages were examined, and their importance to the learning process was shown. We discussed Kohlberg's cognitive-developmental approach to the study of attitudes, values, and morals, which can be used to accelerate the level of moral reasoning in children and adults.

White lays emphasis on the first three years of a child's life, and we discussed Bell's philosophy behind home-based early childhood education — the parent being an important teacher.

In this book, we tried to show that while some children learn best in one way, others cannot learn at all in that way. Children learn by listening and looking, and they express themselves by talking and by doing. Learning problems develop when weaknesses occur in any of these areas. These weaknesses can be remediated if caught

67

early. However, if they are not caught early, they are too severe to remediate; the teacher needs to learn how to work around these weaknesses, approaching the child through his strongest learning channels. When strong and weak channels are combined, often the weaker one can be strengthened.

Teachers should realize that learning takes place through a multisensory approach and plan accordingly. The learning environment should be structured so that the child has an opportunity to explore and discover their best learning modality. We should consider the child from the physiological, psychological, and cultural factors. Programs should be designed that will enable the child to develop in the best possible way.

Even though all children pass through the same developmental and learning stages, it should be kept in mind that individuals progress at their own rate within a particular stage and that a child's background and environment determine the pace at which the child learns.

Opportunities for social interaction should be provided and encouraged, because this process leads to cognitive development. By allowing the child to become self-directed in the learning process, he builds within himself the foundation for a lifetime.

Finally, it is worth noting that children have five senses: sight, hearing, taste, smell, and touch. Why should learning be limited to one or two senses when an individual can learn much more effectively through all their senses and enjoy learning at the same time? Teaching methods need to incorporate all these avenues in order to become more effective.

REFERENCES

Books

Bell, Terrel H. *Your Child's Intellect.* Utah: Olympus Publishing Company, 1973.

Bloom, Benjamin S. (ed.). *Taxonomy of Education Objectives: The Classification of Educational Goals. Handbook 1. Cognitive Domain.* New York: MacKay, 1956.

———— *Stability and Change in Human Characteristics.* New York: John Wiley and Sons, Inc., 1964.

Bruner, Jerome S., et. al. *Studies in Cognitive Growth.* New York: John Wiley and Sons, Inc., 1966A.

———— *Toward A Theory of Instruction.* Cambridge, Mass.: Harvard University Press, 1966B.

Drem, R. C. *Montessori: Her Method and The Movement.* New York: Putnam's Sons, 1974.

Ginsburg, Herbert and Opper, Sylvia. *Piaget's Theory of Intellectual Development: An Introduction.* New Jersey: Prentice Hall, Inc., 1969.

Hainstock, Elizabeth G. *Teaching Montessori in the Home.* New York: Random House, 1968.

Havighurst, Robert J. *Human Development and Education.* New York: David MacKay Co., Inc., 1953.

Klausmeier, Herbert J. and Goodwin, William, 4th ed. *Learning and Human Abilities: Educational Psychology.* New York: Harper and Row, 1975.

Kocher, Marjorie B. *The Montessori's Manual of Cultural Subjects.* Minneapolis: T. S. Denison, 1973.

Moore, Raymond S. *Adventist Education at the Crossroads.* Mountain View, CA: Pacific Press Publishing Association, 1976.

Piaget, Jean. *The Origins of Intelligence in Children.* New York: International Universities Press, Inc., 1952.

Rambush, Nancy M. *Learning How to Learn.* Baltimore: Helicon Press, 1962.

Tyler, R. W. *Basic Principles of Curriculum and Instruction.* Chicago: University of Chicago Press, 1950.

White, Burton L. *The First Three Years of Life.* Englewood Cliffs, NJ: Prentice-Hall, Inc., 1975a.

White, Burton L. and Watts, Jean Carey. *Experience and Environment. Vol. 1.* Englewood Cliffs, NJ: Prentice-Hall, Inc., 1973.

Articles

Berliner, Michael S. "Montessori and Social Development." *Educational Forum* 38 (March 1974) 295-302.

Cole, Diane. "Which Kids Succeed? Some Surprising News." *Family Weekly,* April 11, 1982, p. 7.

Hechinger, Fred M. "Excess is not the way." *New York Times,* October 22, 1972, pp. 77-78.

Kohlberg, Lawrence. "The Cognitive-Developmental Approach to Moral Education." *Phi Delta Kappan* 56 (June 1975) 670-77.

White, Burton L. "Critical Influences in the Origins of Competence." *Merrill-Palmer Quarterly* 21 (No. 4 1975b) 243-66.

———— "Preschool: Has it Worked?" *Compact* 7 (July-August 1973b) 6-7.

———— "When Should Schooling Begin?" *Phi Delta Kappan* 53 (June 1972) 610-12.

INDEX